DELIVERANCE FROM DEMONIC ATTACKS

EVERYTHING YOU NEED TO KNOW ON CASTING OUT DEMONIC SPIRITS

Prayer M. Madueke

BEST-SELLING AUTHOR OF MONITORING SPIRITS & PRAYING WITH THE BLOOD OF JESUS

ISBN: 978-1964584669

All Scripture quotations are taken from the King James Version of the Bible, and used by permission. All emphasis within quotations is the author's additions.

Published by Prayer Publications.
Printed in the United States of America.

4 Free Ebooks

To say a 'Thank You' for purchasing *Deliverance from Demonic Attacks*, I offer these books to you in appreciation. Click or type madueke.com/free-gift in your browser.

Message from the Author

I desire that you succeed, grow, and break free from negativity and obstacles. I want you to flourish, remaining resilient, and untouched by negative influences or challenging circumstances. Because of that, please permit me to introduce two courses that I believe passionately will help you:

1. To break the evil altars and powers of your father's house. The role of altars in the realm of existence is key because altars are meeting places between the physical and the spiritual, between the visible and the invisible.

   Unless a man cuts off the evil flow from the power of his father's house, he will not fulfill his destiny. **Click here** to learn more about **my course** on how to tear down unholy altars and close the enemy's entryways into your life!

2. To help you seamlessly break iron-like problems, illness, delayed marriage, poverty, or any long-standing battle.

   Discover **the transformative power of Christian fasting and prayer**. Remember, Matthew 17:21 teaches us, "But this kind of demon does not go out except by prayer and fasting." Ready to overcome your struggles? **Click here** to learn more about this course.

Embrace the journey ahead with faith, for through prayer, fasting, and the dismantling of evil altars, you shall unlock the doors to spiritual liberation and divine breakthrough. May His grace illuminate your path as you walk towards a life free from bondage.

If you're seeing this from the physical copy, type the link: madueke.com/courses in your browser to view all the courses on my website.

Prayer Madueke
CHRISTIAN AUTHOR

Christian Counseling

We were created for a purpose far greater than mere survival, and God desires us to live a life of true fulfillment.

If you need prayer or counseling or have any other inquiries, please visit the counseling page on my website to find out when I am available for a phone call.

Click or type links.madueke.com/counseling in your browser.

Let's Connect on Youtube

Join me on my YouTube channel, "Prayer M. Madueke," where I share powerful insights, guidance, and prayers for spiritual breakthroughs.

Subscribe today to unlock the secrets of the Kingdom and embrace an abundant life. Let's grow together!

Click or type links.madueke.com/youtube in your browser.

TABLE OF CONTENTS

ONE

THE ORIGIN OF DEMONIC ATTACKS

Satanic attacks came about as a result of the loss of the divine image in which God created man. Man was created holy and pure in heart. He was full of innocence in the garden of Eden. But through the disobedience of Adam and Eve, man fell into sin. He became full of evil and void of holiness. God's word requires holiness.

> And God said, let us make man in our image, after our likeness: and let them have dominion over the fish of the sea, and over the fowl of the air, and over the cattle, and over all the earth, and over every creeping thing that creepeth upon the earth. So, God created man in his own image, in the image of God created he him; male and female created he them

— GENESIS 1:26-27

> And have put on the new man, which is renewed in knowledge after the image of him that created him
>
> — COLOSSIANS 3:10

Man was originally created and destined to have dominion over every creature. He was made in God's image and he was to reign exactly like God among the creatures. And unless you recover your lost divine image through repentance, confession and forsaking of your sins, you can never reign over the creatures in your environment. This was why Paul in his epistles to believers in Colossians encouraged them to put on the new man which is renewed in the knowledge after the image of God who created them.

> And that ye put on the new man, which after God is created in righteousness and true holiness
>
> — EPHESIANS 4:24

> For thou hast made him a little lower than the angels, and hast crowned him with glory and honor. Thou madest him to have dominion over the works of thy hands; thou hast put all things under his feet: All sheep and oxen, yea, and the beasts of the field; The fowl of

> the air, and the fish of the sea, and whatsoever passeth through the paths of the seas. O Lord our Lord, how excellent is thy name in all the earth!
>
> — PSALMS 8:5-9

To the church in Ephesus, a city where idolatry, immorality and cultism were dominant, Paul gave them the same condition. He admonished them to be renewed in their spirit and to put on the new man which is after God. This is to enable them live righteously in the midst of corrupted people in their world. Man was the crown of creation and was invested with glory and honor, just a little lower than angels but sadly, man now lives at the mercy of other creatures. From the beginning, man was made to have dominion over all creation. But unfortunately, the reverse is now the case. Man, now prefers to worship the works of his hands. He bows down to images. He worships, and sacrifices to other gods and elemental forces. He walks after them, swears to them, and looks up to them. He even tries to worship the true God through images.

> Who changed the truth of God into a lie, and worshipped and served the creature more than the Creator, who is blessed for ever. Amen. Being filled with all unrighteousness, fornication, wickedness,

> covetousness, maliciousness; full of envy, murder, debate, deceit, malignity; whisperers, Backbiters, haters of God, despiteful, proud, boasters, inventors of evil things, disobedient to parents, Without understanding, covenantbreakers, without natural affection, implacable, unmerciful: Who knowing the judgment of God, that they which commit such things are worthy of death, not only do the same, but have pleasure in them that do them.
>
> — ROMANS 1:25, 29-32

The Roman Emperors, world leaders, and religious leaders were fully aware of the dire judgment that awaits those who commit sexual immorality, yet they take pleasure in such acts. Today, laws have been passed in many nations allowing people to engage in what God has forbidden. These leaders know that by nature it is wrong for a woman to have carnal knowledge of a fellow woman. Likewise, they know it is wrong for a man to leave the natural use of a woman and be lusting after another man. In spite of this knowledge, our political and religious leaders have chosen to enable and encourage this wrongdoing.

> For this cause God gave them up unto vile affections: for even their women did change the natural use into that which is against nature: And likewise also the

> men, leaving the natural use of the woman, burned in their lust one toward another; men with men working that which is unseemly, and receiving in themselves that recompence of their error which was meet. And even as they did not like to retain God in their knowledge, God gave them over to a reprobate mind, to do those things which are not convenient;
>
> — ROMANS 1:26-28

This is why the world is filled with all manner of unrighteousness, fornication, wickedness, covetousness, maliciousness, envy, murder and deceit. Man is filled with pride, disobedience, and hatred against God and his fellow man. He lacks natural affection and is possessed by demons, causing him to do all manner of horrible things in the name of fighting for human rights.

WHAT PEOPLE DO WHEN THEY LOSE NATURAL AFFECTION

When Adam and Eve lost natural affection by eating the forbidden fruits, they broke the commandment of God. Consequently, they were removed from their comfort zone. They were cursed and brought under the dominion of the devil. Their understanding was darkened and they began to live in disobedience to God's command.

> Having the understanding darkened, being alienated from the life of God through the ignorance that is in them, because of the blindness of their heart.
>
> — EPHESIANS 4:18

> But the natural man receiveth not the things of the Spirit of God: for they are foolishness unto him: neither can he know them, because they are spiritually discerned
>
> — 1 CORINTHIANS 2:14

Adam and Eve lacked true understanding and became alienated from God. They became ignorant because sin blinded their heart spiritually. They began to see the way Satan wanted them to see which was against God's will. Sin deposited inside them an unnatural character which banished holiness from their lives. This made them to do foolish things. Their hearts were deceived and they became desperately wicked.

> The heart is deceitful above all things, and desperately wicked: who can know it?
>
> — JEREMIAH 17:9

The deceitful demons planted in the heart of man made him desperate to do wicked things with no regards to God's word. Furthermore, the conscience of man was defiled, polluted and contaminated. His will was enslaved. This was what made Cain to offer the wrong sacrifice and despise God's counsel. He got angry with his brother Abel who did the right thing by offering a fitting sacrifice to God. He ended up killing Abel and lying to God when confronted. He claimed that he was not his brother's keeper. This was what attracted curses to him. He was cursed to remain a vagabond and a fugitive.

Joseph's brothers hated and envied him. They conspired against him and sold him into slavery. They lied to their father, Jacob, that he was killed by wild animals but God saved Joseph and made him great. Though his brothers later felt guilty and troubled but they never repented. Satan constructed a body inside man called the body of sin, carnal mind or the flesh and internal filthiness.

> Knowing this, that our old man is crucified with him, that the body of sin might be destroyed, that henceforth we should not serve sin
>
> — ROMANS 6:6

> Having therefore these promises, dearly beloved, let us cleanse ourselves from all filthiness of the flesh and spirit, perfecting holiness in the fear of God
>
> — 2 CORINTHIANS 7:1

So, the understanding is that sin is inherited before it is committed. Therefore, sin is referred to as the old man, a dominating tyrant, a hereditary or resident evil. It is the enemy and corrupter of the moral nature (Read Romans 7:14-20; 6:6; Ephesians 4:22; Romans 8:5-8).

Sin lives inside of every man and does not respect your position, certificate or fame. Paul was a Jew who had confidence in flesh. He had the best education and, as was the custom of the Jews, was circumcised on the eight day. He came from the tribe of Benjamin. He was also a Pharisees. Concerning zeal for religion, persecuting the church, and regarding righteousness which is in the law, he was found blameless (Read Acts 26:9-14.)

Despite the above qualities, he was messed up, disgraced and brought to nothing by sin. From his youthful age, he was deceived and diverted from his divinely-ordained purpose. He became prone to committing errors. In midst of confusion and deceit, he couldn't do the right thing even when he wanted. In his helpless and hopeless captivity, he succumbed to sin. Satan used him to commit evil acts in Jerusalem. He entered into places of worship and arrested many saints. He got them locked up in prisons. He had authority to arrest, prosecute and punish the innocent believers of the early church for doing the right thing.

> For we know that the law is spiritual: but I am carnal, sold under sin. For that which I do I allow not: for what I would, that do I not; but what I hate, that do I. If then I do that which I would not, I consent unto the law that it is good. Now then it is no more I that do it, but sin that dwelleth in me. For I know that in me (that is, in my flesh,) dwelleth no good thing: for to will is present with me; but how to perform that which is good I find not. For the good that I would I do not: but the evil which I would not, that I do. Now if I do that I would

> not, it is no more I that do it, but sin that dwelleth in me. I find then a law, that, when I would do good, evil is present with me.
>
> — ROMANS 7:14-21

Though he knew what was right, he was entrapped into doing the opposite by his carnal nature, the sinful man within him. So, he lived under the power of sin, forced to do things he disliked. This is the condition of every man who is not yet repented. He is not to be blamed because he inherited it ever before he was born. Some have tried to escape from this inherited sinful nature on their own but this escape is never complete. They are never completely delivered or freed from sin. Their lives are not complete. They remain helpless captives to sin which always brought them to condemnation.

WHY PEOPLE ARE UNDER DEMONIC ATTACKS

When the children of Israel came out from Egyptian captivity with Egyptian problems, God called them into a healing covenant. A healing covenant demands that the benefactors remain diligent in serving God and obedient to his word. Most people under satanic attacks are either guilty of disobedience to God's word or neglect to resist the devil.

> And said, If thou wilt diligently hearken to the voice of the Lord thy God, and wilt do that which is right in his sight, and wilt give ear to his commandments, and keep all his statutes, I will put none of these diseases upon thee, which I have brought upon the Egyptians: for I am the Lord that healeth thee
>
> — EXODUS 15:26

> Submit yourselves therefore to God. Resist the devil, and he will flee from you
>
> — JAMES 4:7

If you repent of your sins, confess and forsake them, you have to enter into the healing covenant to live holy in obedience to God's word. The devil will try to bring you under his control with problems but you are called to resist him. While resisting him, you must keep God's word. Be diligent hearing His voice. Do what is right in His sight. Keep His commandments even under demonic attacks. When you prove to God that, no matter what, you are determined to follow Him and keep His statutes, He will deliver you from every demonic attack.

> Who forgiveth all thine iniquities; who healeth all thy diseases
>
> — PSALM 103:3

> My son, attend to my words; incline thine ear unto my sayings. Let them not depart from thine eyes; keep them in the midst of thine heart. For they are life unto those that find them, and health to all their flesh
>
> — PROVERBS 4:20-22

In order to enjoy complete deliverance and freedom from satanic attacks, your iniquities must have been forgiven. It is wrong to seek for complete deliverance or freedom from demonic attacks when you are not ready to give up your iniquities. You must attend to God's word and reject anything that contradicts His word. You must not seek for anything, be it blessing, freedom, healing, deliverance or position, outside

God's word. You must be careful to not seek for anything that is not consistent with God's word. You must be steadfast in observing and attending God's word. You must persistently refuse to go against His word in trying to get anything here on earth.

> When the even was come, they brought unto him many that were possessed with devils: and he cast out the spirits with his word, and healed all that were sick: That it might be fulfilled which was spoken by Esaias the prophet, saying, Himself took our infirmities, and bare our sicknesses
>
> — MATTHEW 8:16-17

> Who his own self bare our sins in his own body on the tree, that we, being dead to sins, should live unto righteousness: by whose stripes ye were healed
>
> — 1 PETER 2:24

If you truly wish to obtain complete freedom from satanic attacks and be able to keep and enjoy it in order to fulfil God's purpose for you on earth, you must avoid the ways of the wicked. To enjoy the redemptive sacrifice of Christ on the cross, you must keep His commandments. Of a truth, He bore our griefs and carried our sorrows but you can only reap the benefits if you stay away from iniquities. Though He was wounded for our transgressions, bruised for our iniquities, chastised for our peace and though by His stripes, He paid for our healing, you can only enjoy the above if you maintain total obedience to His word

> And ye shall serve the Lord your God, and he shall bless thy bread, and thy water; and I will take sickness away from the midst of thee. There shall nothing cast their young, nor be barren, in thy land: the number of thy days I will fulfil. I will send my fear before thee, and will destroy all the people to whom thou shalt come, and I will make all thine enemies turn their backs unto thee. And I will send hornets before thee, which shall drive out the Hivite, the Canaanite, and the Hittite, from before thee. I will not drive them out from before thee in one year; lest the land become desolate, and the beast of the field multiply against thee.

— EXODUS 23:25-29

If out of compassion by His mercy, you received healing, deliverance and freedom from any demonic oppression while you are still a sinner, you are called to repent, confess and forsake your sins in order to maintain your freedom. Gifted ministers of God or prayerful believers may be used to bring about your deliverance but you must obey God's word if you truly wish to remain delivered. The condition to keep the Israelites safe from satanic torment, oppression and bondage is that they must serve God and not the devil. Serving both God and Satan is impossible.. You are called to serve God after repentance and to remain faithful in His service to in order to remain free from satanic oppression. You may experience material blessings and freedom from diseases and satanic oppression but if you fail to remain holy, your blessings and freedom will not last. If your blessings are from God, there will be no sorrow in them. You cannot die young because nothing in God's hands shall cast their young.

> Wherefore it shall come to pass, if ye hearken to these judgments, and keep, and do them, that the Lord thy God shall keep unto thee the covenant and the mercy which he sware unto thy fathers: And he will love thee, and bless thee, and multiply thee: he will also bless the fruit of thy womb, and the fruit of thy land, thy corn, and thy wine, and thine oil, the increase of thy kine, and the flocks of thy sheep, in the land which he sware unto thy fathers to give thee. Thou shalt be blessed above all people: there shall not be male or female barren among you, or among your cattle. And the Lord will take away from thee all sickness, and will put none

> of the evil diseases of Egypt, which thou knowest, upon thee; but will lay them upon all them that hate thee.
>
> — DEUTERONOMY 7:12-15

Barrenness, lack and premature death are contrary to God's promises for His obedient children. Though the devil may attempt to use these afflictions to attack believers but he must be resisted until he flees. God is ever ready to destroy anyone who stands in the way of true believers. Any power or personality that vows to block the way of a true child of God will be destroyed. This is God's promise. On the battle field of life, true children of God can be attacked but God promised to weaken and turn back their attackers. God will send hornets before a determined believer to drive nations of demons away.

Your enemies may resist and try to stay in order to torment you forever but as you remain faithful to God's word, they will flee. Your problem may be poverty, pestilence, sickness, shameful situation, late marriage, barrenness or a nameless disease, God will deliver you and give you complete freedom if you enter into a covenant of healing with Him. Covenant people of God cannot be defeated or destroyed by demonic attacks as long as they remain faithful to the end. If you keep God's covenant and remain loyal to his word, no evil judgment will be upheld in your life. The promise of God to His covenant children is to bless, multiply and make them fruitful in everything they do. Your expectation as an obedient child of God is to be blessed above others in everything you lay your hands to do. God also promised to take away diseases and all manner of problems from His faithful covenant children.

TWO

EXERCISING SUPERNATURAL AUTHORITY

Jesus came to this world with heavenly authority and the full backing of God, His father. With that authority, He healed an impotent man who was bound in a place by demons for thirty-eight years. When Jesus encountered this man, he had no hope of deliverance. Every door to deliverance, healing and liberty was closed against him. He was denied every human help.

> In these lay a great multitude of impotent folk, of blind, halt, withered, waiting for the moving of the water. For an angel went down at a certain season into the pool, and troubled the water: whosoever then first after the troubling of the water stepped in was made

> whole of whatsoever disease he had. And a certain man was there, which had an infirmity thirty and eight years. When Jesus saw him lie, and knew that he had been now a long time in that case, he saith unto him, wilt thou be made whole?
>
> — JOHN 5:3-6

He was not alone in that situation but to him, deliverance was no longer possible because there was no light at the end of the tunnel of suffering. You may think that you are alone in this battle of life but you are wrong. Jesus is around you now and closer to you than the blood in you. Angels couldn't help this impotent man, neither could even his blood relations. They all abandoned him but one day, just like today, Jesus appeared on the battlefield of his life.

> The impotent man answered him, Sir, I have no man, when the water is troubled, to put me into the pool: but while I am coming, another steppeth down before me. Jesus saith unto him, Rise, take up thy bed, and walk. And immediately the man was made whole, and took up his bed, and walked: and on the same day was the sabbath
>
> — JOHN 5:7-9

For thirty-eight years, nobody bothered about him but that day, Jesus asked him a simple question, wilt thou be made whole? Instead of answering the question, the impotent man began to tell stories, complain, find faults and shift blames. He spoke about how he was abandoned for thirty-eight years. With authority from heaven, Jesus commanded him to rise, take up thy bed and walk out from the bondage of impotence and demonic attacks completely.

What happened here? Jesus used his authority, even thought it was on a sabbath day and immediately the man was made whole. He got out of bed and walked.

> And Jesus went about all Galilee, teaching in their synagogues, and preaching the gospel of the kingdom, and healing all manner of sickness and all manner of disease among the people. And his fame went throughout all Syria: and they brought unto him all sick people that were taken with divers diseases and torments, and those which were possessed with devils, and those which were lunatick, and those that had the palsy; and he healed them. And there followed him great multitudes of people from Galilee, and from Decapolis, and from Jerusalem, and from Judaea, and from beyond Jordan.
>
> — MATTHEW 4:23

When He came in contact with people with all manner of diseases, people who were possessed with devils, lunatics and those with palsy, he healed them. The demons in them left when they heard the word of God. With His authority, Jesus cleansed lepers, cast out demons that came from tombs to possess people. With the same authority, He opened the eyes of the blinds, stretched forth withered hands, fed the hungry, walked on top of the marine kingdom (water) and terminated demonic oppression.

> And there was in their synagogue a man with an unclean spirit; and he cried out, Saying, let us alone; what have we to do with thee, thou Jesus of Nazareth? art thou come to destroy us? I know thee who thou art, the Holy One of God. And Jesus rebuked him, saying, hold thy peace, and come out of him. And when the unclean spirit had torn him, and cried with a loud voice, he came out of him.
>
> — MARK 1:23-26

As He went into the synagogue, he saw a man possessed by demons.. The spirit inside the man cried out and accused Jesus of intending to destroy it. Unclean spirits recognize Jesus as a man with the power to destroy them. With authority, Jesus rebuked the unclean spirit and commanded it to come out. The unclean spirit immediately came out and the man was freed from demonic attacks. With authority, Jesus terminated plagues, stopped storms, halted evil winds, broke chains of bondage and delivered people who were about to die. A lady who suffered from a bleeding disorder for twelve years was healed by Jesus..

> And it came to pass the day after, that he went into a city called Nain; and many of his disciples went with him, and much people. Now when he came nigh to the gate of the city, behold, there was a dead man carried out, the only son of his mother, and she was a widow: and much people of the city was with her. And when the Lord saw her, he had compassion on her, and said unto her, Weep not. And he came and touched the bier: and they that bare him stood still. And he said, Young man, I say unto thee, Arise. And he that was dead sat up, and began to speak. And he delivered him to his mother.

— LUKE 7:11-15

He disgraced the kingdom of darkness by confronting and conquering death. After teaching in Capernaum, He entered the city of Nain through the gate. Right in the gate of the city with his disciples with much people followed Him, He saw another company of people in the gate. This group of people, mainly youths in the front and few elders with much people coming out of the city also. They carried a dead body, a young man, the only son of his mother who was also a widow. There was a clash in the gate between Jesus company and the company that carried the dead body. When Jesus saw how devasted the woman was without hope of having another child, He had compassion on her. He quickly told the woman to stop weeping. The woman was not touched by that word because she had heard such words many times from people who consoled her.

But when Jesus says to you, weep not, that is the end and that is what He is telling you now. He approached the people carrying the dead body and touched the bier and they stood still. Everything will stand still until you are completely delivered out of every satanic attack today. Jesus with authority said, "Young man, I say unto thee, Arise."

And he that was dead, you that everyone believed that you can never make it will arise in the midst of defeated people and make it from today.

The young man left dead people, failed people sat up and began to talk.

YOU CAN USE YOUR AUTHORITY

The same anointing that God gave to His son the LORD Jesus is made available to all His followers. Acts 10:38 says, "How God anointed Jesus of Nazareth with the Holy Ghost and with power: who went about doing good, and healing all that were oppressed of the devil: for God is with Him." The same Spirit that God used in anointing Jesus is inside of every believer that receives Him as Lord and personal savior.

> But if the Spirit of him that raised up Jesus from the dead dwell in you, he that raised up Christ from the dead shall also quicken your mortal bodies by his Spirit that dwelleth in you
>
> — ROMANS 8:11

> What? know ye not that your body is the temple of the Holy Ghost which is in you, which ye have of God, and ye are not your own?
>
> — 1 CORINTHIANS 6:19

If you have the Spirit of Christ, nothing shall be impossible to you because God's Spirit is the same as God and with God nothing shall be impossible. With the Spirit of God in you, living in your body which is His temple, you can cast out devils, stop satanic activities and oppression anywhere. When Jesus was leaving this earth, He didn't go with the power to cast out demons. There are no demons or evil spirits in heaven so He gave his followers the power to cast out demons, tread on serpents and scorpions.

> Behold, I give unto you power to tread on serpents and scorpions, and over all the power of the enemy: and nothing shall by any means hurt you
>
> — LUKE 10:19

> And Jesus came and spake unto them, saying, all power is given unto me in heaven and in earth
>
> — MATTHEW 28:18

Before He ascended into heaven, He called his disciples together and said, "All power is given unto me in heaven and in earth". In Luke 9:1, He gave them power and authority over demons and to cure diseases.

> Verily, verily, I say unto you, He that believeth on me, the works that I do shall he do also; and greater works than these shall he do; because I go unto my Father. And whatsoever ye shall ask in my name, that will I do,

> that the Father may be glorified in the Son. If ye shall ask anything in my name, I will do it.
>
> — JOHN 14:12-14

All you need now as a child of God is to believe that through His power by His Spirit in you, you can cast out demons. Believe that you can be freed from satanic attacks by the power of God in you. If only you believe, you can cast out evil spirits, rebuke demons and do greater work than Jesus did. Whatever you ask in prayer using the name of Christ, you will get it.

> Verily I say unto you, Whatsoever ye shall bind on earth shall be bound in heaven: and whatsoever ye shall loose on earth shall be loosed in heaven.Again, I say unto you, that if two of you shall agree on earth as touching anything that they shall ask, it shall be done for them of my Father which is in heaven
>
> — MATTHEW 18:18-19

Christ has given you the power to bind anything here on earth and have it bound in heaven. Similarly, you can release anything here on earth and have released in heaven. Anything you say will come to pass as long as you have faith and believe.

THREE

UNMASKING THE POWERS OF DARKNESS

The existence of demons is not a myth, nor are they mere figments of human imagination. They are ancient beings, fallen from grace, and deeply entrenched in the affairs of the world. To understand their origin is to comprehend their operations, for without knowledge, many remain entrapped in cycles of spiritual bondage. The Bible provides an undeniable record of their beginning, their nature, and their mission to resist the will of God.

Before their rebellion, demons were not what they are today. They were once glorious angels, created with divine beauty and purpose. The Scriptures tell us that these beings once stood in the presence of God, fulfilling their celestial assignments.

> And the angels which kept not their first estate, but left their own habitation, he hath reserved in everlasting chains under darkness unto the judgment of the great day.
>
> — JUDE 6

> For if God spared not the angels that sinned, but cast them down to hell, and delivered them into chains of darkness, to be reserved unto judgment;
>
> — 2 PETER 2:4

They were radiant, magnificent, and perfectly made, dwelling in the very courts of heaven. Among them was one who stood above all others, Lucifer, the anointed cherub. His name meant "light-bearer," and he shone with an unmatched brilliance.

> Thou art the anointed cherub that covereth; and I have set thee so: thou wast upon the holy mountain of God; thou hast walked up and down in the midst of the stones of fire. Thou wast perfect in thy ways from the day that thou wast created, till iniquity was found in thee.
>
> — EZEKIEL 28:14-15

However, pride became his downfall. He wanted more than what he got.. He desired the throne of the Most High, yearning to ascend above the stars and be like the Almighty (Isaiah 14:12-14). This desire led to his rebellion, and with him, a third of heaven's angels followed in his treachery.

> And his tail drew the third part of the stars of heaven, and did cast them to the earth: and the dragon stood before the woman which was ready to be delivered, for to devour her child as soon as it was born.
>
> — REVELATION 12:4

Their once-glorious status was stripped away, and they were cast down from their heavenly estate into a state of eternal condemnation.

THE STRUCTURE OF THE DEMONIC REALM – A HIERARCHICAL SYSTEM OF WICKEDNESS

To wage effective warfare against the forces of darkness, one must first understand their leader. The Bible ascribes numerous names to Satan, each revealing a different aspect of his character and operations. These names provide insights into his tactics and the areas he seeks to manipulate:

- **The Devil** (Jude 9) – The chief of all fallen spirits.
- **Satan** (Luke 10:18) – The adversary and opposer of God's people.
- **The Accuser** (Revelation 12:10) – Constantly bringing charges against believers.
- **The Adversary** (1 Peter 5:8) – Roaming like a roaring lion, seeking whom to devour.
- **Abaddon/Apollyon** (Revelation 9:11) – The destroyer, leading masses into destruction.
- **Beelzebub** (Matthew 12:24) – Lord of demons.
- **The Dragon** (Revelation 12:3) – Symbol of immense power and deception.

- **The Father of Lies** (John 8:44) – Master of deception and falsehood.
- **Lucifer** (Isaiah 14:12) – The fallen morning star.
- **The Prince of This World** (John 14:30) – Ruler of worldly systems and influences.
- **The Wicked One** (2 Thessalonians 2:8) – Manifesting evil and wickedness on the earth.

These names and titles are not merely symbolic; they reflect the very nature of the demonic hierarchy and their strategies against mankind.

Following their expulsion from heaven, Satan and his angels found a new dominion. Their first abode was in the Garden of Eden, where the serpent cunningly deceived mankind, setting in motion the cycle of sin and destruction.

> Now the serpent was more subtil than any beast of the field which the LORD God had made. And he said unto the woman, Yea, hath God said, Ye shall not eat of every tree of the garden? And the woman said unto the serpent, We may eat of the fruit of the trees of the garden: But of the fruit of the tree which is in the midst of the garden, God hath said, Ye shall not eat of

> it, neither shall ye touch it, lest ye die. And the serpent said unto the woman, Ye shall not surely die: For God doth know that in the day ye eat thereof, then your eyes shall be opened, and ye shall be as gods, knowing good and evil.
>
> — GENESIS 3:1-5

This was the beginning of their relentless war against humanity.

Ezekiel 28:16 describes how Lucifer, once perfect in his ways, became filled with iniquity and corrupted himself through pride and violence. He defiled holy places and became the father of corruption. His rebellion did not only affect himself but also led countless angels into the abyss of wickedness. The same Ezekiel passage describes him as a "terrorist," a fitting depiction of his influence in the world today, bringing chaos, destruction, and fear wherever he operates.

Demons do not operate in disarray; they follow a structured system. Ephesians 6:12 speaks of "principalities, powers, rulers of darkness, and spiritual wickedness in high places." This reveals a carefully arranged kingdom of darkness with specific roles and assignments:

1. **Principalities** – High-ranking demonic forces that govern territories and regions.

2. **Powers** – Entities influencing political, economic, and social systems.

3. **Rulers of Darkness** – Spirits spreading deception, falsehood, and moral decay.

4. **Spiritual Wickedness in High Places** – Demonic activities infiltrating religious institutions, leading people astray.

This hierarchy ensures the continuation of Satan's agenda on earth, influencing leaders, cultures, and even religious establishments to propagate deception.

Scripture warns of the coming of the Antichrist and the False Prophet, two powerful demonic manifestations that will deceive many in the end times.

> And I stood upon the sand of the sea, and saw a beast rise up out of the sea, having seven heads and ten horns, and upon his horns ten crowns, and upon his heads the name of blasphemy. And the beast which I saw was like unto a leopard, and his feet were as the feet of a bear, and his mouth as the mouth of a lion: and the dragon gave him his power, and his seat, and great authority. And I saw one of his heads as it were wounded to death; and his deadly wound was healed: and all the world wondered after the beast. And they

worshipped the dragon which gave power unto the beast: and they worshipped the beast, saying, Who is like unto the beast? who is able to make war with him? And there was given unto him a mouth speaking great things and blasphemies; and power was given unto him to continue forty and two months. And he opened his mouth in blasphemy against God, to blaspheme his name, and his tabernacle, and them that dwell in heaven. And it was given unto him to make war with the saints, and to overcome them: and power was given him over all kindreds, and tongues, and nations. And all that dwell upon the earth shall worship him, whose names are not written in the book of life of the Lamb slain from the foundation of the world. If any man have an ear, let him hear. He that leadeth into captivity shall go into captivity: he that killeth with the sword must be killed with the sword. Here is the patience and the faith of the saints. And I beheld another beast coming up out of the earth; and he had two horns like a lamb, and he spake as a dragon. And he exerciseth all the power of the first beast before him, and causeth the earth and them which dwell therein to worship the first beast, whose deadly wound was healed. And he doeth great wonders, so that he maketh fire come down from heaven on the earth in the sight of men, And deceiveth them that dwell on the earth by the means of those miracles which he had power to do in the sight of the beast; saying to them that dwell on the

> earth, that they should make an image to the beast, which had the wound by a sword, and did live. And he had power to give life unto the image of the beast, that the image of the beast should both speak, and cause that as many as would not worship the image of the beast should be killed. And he causeth all, both small and great, rich and poor, free and bond, to receive a mark in their right hand, or in their foreheads: And that no man might buy or sell, save he that had the mark, or the name of the beast, or the number of his name. Here is wisdom. Let him that hath understanding count the number of the beast: for it is the number of a man; and his number is Six hundred threescore and six.
>
> — REVELATION 13:1-18

The Antichrist will emerge as a political leader, deceiving nations through false peace and miraculous wonders. The False Prophet, appearing as a religious figure, will direct worship towards the beast, leading millions into eternal damnation.

Daniel 7:8-11 describes the blasphemous nature of the Antichrist, while 2 Thessalonians 2:9 reveals that he will perform lying wonders. These demonic figures are already preparing the world for their rule through deception, lawlessness, and counterfeit miracles.

The goal of demonic forces is clear:

- **To steal, kill, and destroy** (John 10:10)
- **To deceive nations** (Revelation 12:9)
- **To hinder the work of God** (Daniel 10:13)
- **To oppress and possess individuals** (Luke 8:30-33)
- **To wage war against the saints** (Revelation 13:7)

Understanding their tactics is crucial in standing against them. Believers must be equipped with spiritual knowledge, covered in prayer, and armed with the Word of God to resist these forces.

The origin of demons is a solemn reminder of the consequences of pride and rebellion. The same spirit that caused Lucifer to fall is at work today, seeking to corrupt and ensnare as many as possible. Yet, as believers, we are not powerless. Jesus Christ has given us authority to trample upon serpents and scorpions, and to overcome all the power of the enemy.

> Behold, I give unto you power to tread on serpents and scorpions, and over all the power of the enemy: and nothing shall by any means hurt you.

— LUKE 10:19

THE OPERATIONAL SYSTEM OF SATAN

Every organization, including every kingdom, has a modus operandi, that is a structured way in which it operates. This is also true of the kingdom of darkness. Understanding how Satan operates is essential for developing spiritual intelligence. The Bible clearly reveals his operational system, helping believers to be aware and equipped against his schemes.

Ephesians 6:11 states:

> "Put on the whole armor of God, that ye may be able to stand against the wiles of the devil."

The word "wiles" refers to schemes or devices, meaning Satan has a structured plan for destruction. He does not operate randomly but follows a strategic blueprint to achieve his goals.

2 Corinthians 2:11 reinforces this understanding:

> "Lest Satan should get an advantage of us: for we are not ignorant of his devices."

This passage emphasizes the importance of recognizing the enemy's strategies to avoid being deceived or overpowered.

By examining Satan's activities in Scripture, we gain insight into his methods. The following are key aspects of his operation:

1. Satan and Demons Fight

Revelation 12:7 says:

> "And there was war in heaven: Michael and his angels fought against the dragon; and the dragon fought and his angels."

Fighting is part of Satan's character and strategy. He wages war against God's purposes and those who align with Him.

2. Satan Hinders and Resists

1 Thessalonians 2:18 states:

> "Wherefore we would have come unto you, even I Paul, once and again; but Satan hindered us."

This verse shows that Satan actively resists and obstructs the plans and progress of God's people.

3. Satan Steals, Kills, and Destroys

John 10:10 reveals:

> "The thief cometh not, but for to steal, and to kill, and to destroy."

Satan is described as a thief who seeks to rob people of their blessings, destroy their lives, and bring ruin.

Matthew 13:19 further illustrates Satan's theft:

> "When anyone heareth the word of the kingdom, and understandeth it not, then cometh the wicked one, and catcheth away that which was sown in his heart."

Satan is capable of stealing the truth from people's hearts, preventing them from growing in faith.

4. Satan and Demons Lie

John 8:44 states:

> "Ye are of your father the devil, and the lusts of your father ye will do. He was a murderer from the beginning, and abode not in the truth, because there

> is no truth in him. When he speaketh a lie, he speaketh of his own: for he is a liar, and the father of it."

Lying is Satan's default nature. He deceives by distorting truth and spreading falsehood.

5. Satan Disguises Himself

2 Corinthians 11:14 warns:

> "And no marvel; for Satan himself is transformed into an angel of light."

Satan uses disguise to deceive people, appearing as something good when his intentions are evil.

6. Satan is a Master Deceiver

2 Corinthians 11:3 states:

> "But I fear, lest by any means, as the serpent beguiled Eve through his subtilty, so your minds should be corrupted from the simplicity that is in Christ."

Satan's deception is subtle, leading people away from the truth of Christ.

Revelation 12:9 confirms the extent of his deception:

> "And the great dragon was cast out, that old serpent, called the Devil, and Satan, which deceiveth the whole world."

His deception is not limited to individuals but extends globally.

7. Satan is the Accuser of the Brethren

Revelation 12:10 describes Satan as the accuser:

> "For the accuser of our brethren is cast down, which accused them before our God day and night."

Satan constantly seeks to bring accusations against believers, attempting to condemn and discourage them.

Among all of Satan's operations, deception is the most pronounced. It is his primary weapon against humanity.

What Does It Mean to Deceive?

Intentionally leading another person astray from the truth is what it means to deceive.. Deception is Satan's primary tool to lead people away from God's truth and into bondage.

As we navigate these perilous times, we must remain vigilant, discerning, and steadfast in faith. The battle is real, but victory is certain for those who stand firm in the power of God's might. The forces of darkness may be formidable, but they are not invincible. In Christ, we have the ultimate victory.

FOUR

THE CHAINS OF INCURABLE SICKNESS AND DISEASES

Throughout history, people have been sick and had other problems in their lives that caused them pain, sorrow, and hopelessness. A lot of people look for solutions in medicine, science, or even the supernatural, but the real cause of these problems lies in spiritual realms. Behind the curtain of the real world, a fight goes on that can't be seen. In this battle, evil forces are trying to control, torture, and destroy. That's why it is very important to understand the source of incurable diseases and how to break free from their grip.

The world often attributes sickness to natural causes like bacteria, viruses, genetics, but Scripture reveals that the origin of many diseases is disobedience to God's word. From the beginning, God set forth laws that, when followed, bring health and life, but when broken, they invite destruction.

> "But it shall come to pass, if thou wilt not hearken unto the voice of the Lord thy God, to observe to do all his commandments and his statutes which I command thee this day; that all these curses shall come upon thee, and overtake thee."
>
> — DEUTERONOMY 28:15

Among these curses are sicknesses, plagues, and mental torment, which result from rebellion against God. When man turns away from the Creator, he opens himself to the oppression of the enemy.

Satan, the arch-enemy of God, thrives in deception, affliction, and destruction. He seeks to sow pain among those who stray from God's presence, using sickness as a weapon against humanity.

> "So went Satan forth from the presence of the Lord, and smote Job with sore boils from the sole of his foot unto his crown."
>
> — JOB 2:7

> "The thief cometh not, but for to steal, and to kill, and to destroy."
>
> — JOHN 10:10

Satan's primary goal is to separate man from God through sin and suffering. Every act of disobedience, every engagement with darkness, and every rejection of divine truth strengthens the enemy's grip, leading to physical and spiritual affliction.

Many unknowingly invite demonic oppression into their lives by engaging in practices that are gateways for spirits of affliction. These include:

- **Sinful lifestyles** – Living in rebellion against God's word invites spiritual attacks.
- **Consultation with familiar spirits** – Seeking guidance from psychics, astrologers, or spiritists opens the door to demonic influence.
- **Witchcraft and occult practices** – Engaging in spells, incantations, or secret societies binds individuals to spiritual oppression.
- **Initiation or dedication to dark powers** – Any form of covenant or alliance with the forces of darkness grants demons legal access to afflict the body and soul.

> "Neither give place to the devil."
>
> — EPHESIANS 4:27

> "When the unclean spirit is gone out of a man, he walketh through dry places, seeking rest, and findeth none. Then he saith, I will return into my house from whence I came out; and when he is come, he findeth it empty, swept, and garnished."
>
> — MATTHEW 12:43-45

These scriptures make it clear that without true repentance and renunciation of all ties to darkness, demonic oppression will persist, bringing along more affliction and torment.

Deliverance from the grip of demonic affliction is never automatic rather it requires an intentional and radical commitment to God. Repentance is the first and most critical step.

> "Submit yourselves therefore to God. Resist the devil, and he will flee from you."
>
> — JAMES 4:7

To experience total healing and deliverance:

1. **Repent genuinely** – Confess and renounce every sin, closing every door of access to the enemy.
2. **Destroy all demonic properties** – Get rid of any items linked to the occult, witchcraft, or sinful practices.
3. **Commit to God wholeheartedly** – True deliverance comes when one dedicates their life completely to Christ.
4. **Engage in spiritual warfare** – Stand firm against the enemy with the Word of God and fervent prayer.

> "And Samuel spake unto all the house of Israel, saying, If ye do return unto the Lord with all your hearts, then put away the strange gods and Ashtaroth from among you, and prepare your hearts unto the Lord, and serve him only: and he will deliver you out of the hand of the Philistines. Then the children of Israel did put away Baalim and Ashtaroth, and served the Lord only."

— 1 SAMUEL 7:3-4

Just as the Israelites had to remove foreign gods to be delivered, so must we remove every evil attachment from our lives.

Holding on to sin or demonic objects gives Satan a legal right to stay and afflict.

> "And many that believed came, and confessed, and shewed their deeds. Many of them also which used curious arts brought their books together, and burned them before all men: and they counted the price of them, and found it fifty thousand pieces of silver."
>
> — ACTS 19:18-19

The early Christians demonstrated true repentance by burning all objects associated with sorcery and witchcraft, refusing to give the devil any foothold.

Many believers struggle with persistent sickness and oppression because they unknowingly harbor demonic tokens in their homes and lives. As long as one keeps:

- Sin and unforgiveness in their heart
- Occultic books, charms, amulets, or talismans
- Ritualistic objects or clothing linked to dark powers
- Engages in hidden sinful practices

Satan will have a legal right to remain and afflict.

Healing and deliverance are available, but they come at the price of total surrender to God. God's power is limitless, and His desire is to see His children walk in divine health and wholeness.

> "If the Son therefore shall make you free, ye shall be free indeed."
>
> — JOHN 8:36

FIVE

WALKING IN TOTAL DELIVERANCE

It takes knowledge and revelation to operate effectively in the Kingdom of God, as this is a kingdom governed by light. Therefore, it is essential that believers are equipped with the necessary understanding.

During my study in preparation for this section, I discovered something striking: Jesus never sent out His disciples or apostles on any mission without first ensuring they had a thorough understanding of the structure and system of darkness. It is dangerous to engage in any aspect of Kingdom work while being ignorant, especially regarding the devices of the enemy. That is why I urge you to open your hearts and spirits to receive this teaching without distraction.

Satan has two primary objectives:

1. **Dominion** – He seeks the authority that was originally given to mankind.

2. **Transgenerational Allegiance** – He desires loyalty that spans across generations.

Behind all forms of evil, oppression, and destruction, Satan's ultimate goal remains the same: to gain dominion and secure perpetual allegiance from individuals, families, and territories. This understanding helps demystify his strategies and reveals that patterns such as ancestral altars, curses, and negative cycles exist to ensure generational continuity of satanic influence.

Patterns manifest in various forms, including:

- Family-wide occurrences of anger, theft, irresponsibility, or untimely death.

- Regional strongholds that influence entire communities.

- Superstitions and traditions designed to enforce allegiance to demonic spirits.

Satan's approach is methodical. He seeks to keep people bound in negative patterns, ensuring that his dominion and influence continue. Understanding this is key to breaking free from such bondages.

One of Satan's primary tactics is to create problems in people's lives, be it barrenness, financial hardship, sickness, or oppression, and then offer a false solution that leads them back into spiritual bondage. He manipulates circumstances to force individuals into seeking alternatives outside of God's provision. This is how many of our forefathers unknowingly entered into covenants with demonic entities, often in exchange for protection, fertility, or victory in battles.

The missionaries who brought the gospel were sincere, but their emphasis was largely on salvation without addressing the spiritual legalities of deliverance. As a result, many believers experienced setbacks, not because Christianity was weak, but because they lacked the full revelation necessary to legally break free from the influence of ancestral covenants.

We must embrace the complete gospel, one that not only brings salvation but also provides the spiritual intelligence necessary to navigate these legalities. The key to overcoming the enemy's influence is through revelation and truth.

> So if the Son liberates you [makes you free men], then you are really and unquestionably free.
>
> — JOHN 8:36

Additionally, Obadiah 1:17 states:

> But upon Mount Zion shall be deliverance, and there shall be holiness; and the house of Jacob shall possess their possessions.

Deliverance is not merely an event; it is a process, a journey that requires obedience, faith, and a steadfast commitment to God. Many people receive temporary relief from demonic oppression but fail to walk in sustained victory because they neglect the steps necessary to maintain their deliverance. True deliverance is not only about casting out demons but about keeping them out and living in divine dominion.

1. Step 1: Obedience to God

> "Now if you obey me fully and keep my covenant, then out of all nations you will be my treasured possession."
>
> — EXODUS 19:5

Obedience to God is the foundation for maintaining a life free from demonic bondage. Many people seek deliverance but are unwilling to submit to God's commands. Without obedience, any deliverance received is temporary. Disobedience opens doors for demonic influences, allowing the enemy legal grounds to operate in one's life.

Biblical Foundations of Obedience:

- God's blessings are tied to obedience (Deuteronomy 28:1-14).
- Disobedience brings curses, sickness, and affliction (Deuteronomy 28:15-68).
- Obedience leads to divine protection and favor (Joshua 1:5-8, 2 Chronicles 15:1-2).
- God requires complete surrender, not partial obedience (1 Samuel 15:22).
- A life of holiness and purity is expected of every believer (1 Peter 1:14-16, Hebrews 5:8-9).

Obedience is not just about following God's laws; it is about developing an intimate relationship with Him. When you walk in obedience, you align yourself with the will of God, making it impossible for the enemy to find a foothold in your life.

Step 2: Entering into a Healing Covenant with God

> "If you listen carefully to the LORD your God and do what is right in his eyes, if you pay attention to his commands and keep all his decrees, I will not bring on you any of the diseases I brought on the Egyptians, for I am the LORD, who heals you."
>
> — EXODUS 15:26

Deliverance and divine health go hand in hand. When you enter into a covenant with God through faith in His promises, you position yourself to live in divine healing and protection. Many believers struggle with sickness and demonic oppression because they fail to enforce their covenant rights in Christ.

Keys to Walking in Divine Health:

- Serve the Lord wholeheartedly (Exodus 23:25-31).
- Keep God's commandments and align with His principles (Deuteronomy 7:12-15).
- Recognize sickness as an attack of the enemy and resist it through faith and prayer.

Walking in divine health is a covenant, and like all covenants, it requires faithfulness and commitment. If you desire complete deliverance, you must embrace God's promises and reject the lies of the enemy that suggest sickness is inevitable.

Step 3: Imitate Christ in Deliverance

> "And you shall know the truth, and the truth shall make you free."
>
> — JOHN 8:32

Jesus Christ set the perfect example of deliverance ministry. His earthly ministry was marked by healing the sick, casting out demons, and setting the oppressed free. To walk in full deliverance, we must follow His footsteps.

Jesus' Deliverance Ministry:

- He healed by rebuking the devil (Matthew 4:23-24).
- He cast out demons with authority (Matthew 8:23-34, 9:32-33, 12:28-29).
- He empowered His disciples to do the same (Matthew 10:1, 8, Luke 9:1, 10:18-20).

- He promised believers the same power (John 14:12-14, Matthew 18:18-19).

Jesus performed deliverance through the power of the Holy Spirit, and that same Spirit dwells in us (Romans 8:11, 1 Corinthians 6:19). We are not helpless against demonic oppression; we have been given authority to cast out spirits and heal the sick.

Step 4: Exercising Your Authority Over Evil Spirits

Many believers live in unnecessary bondage because they do not understand their authority in Christ. The power of God is available to every child of God, but it must be exercised through faith.

> "These signs will accompany those who believe: In my name they will drive out demons; they will speak in new tongues; they will place their hands on sick people, and they will get well."
>
> — MARK 16:17-18

Keys to Exercising Authority:

1. **Know your identity in Christ** – You are seated with Christ in heavenly places (Ephesians 2:6).

2. **Use the name of Jesus** – The name of Jesus carries power over every demonic force (Philippians 2:9-11).

3. **Be filled with the Holy Spirit** – The Spirit of God empowers you to overcome the enemy (Acts 1:8).

4. **Speak the Word of God with boldness** – The Word is a spiritual weapon against darkness (Ephesians 6:17, Matthew 4:4-10).

5. **Live a consecrated life** – Holiness ensures that the enemy has no legal ground in your life (James 4:7, 1 Peter 5:8-9).

When you fully embrace the authority given to you as a believer, no demon, sickness, or oppression can have power over you.

Deliverance is not a one-time event; it is a continuous process that requires spiritual vigilance, faith, and obedience to God. Many people experience deliverance but fail to walk in sustained freedom because they revert to sinful lifestyles, neglect prayer, and allow fear and doubt to creep in. To maintain your deliverance, you must:

- Stay in the Word of God daily.
- Live a life of holiness and obedience.
- Guard your mind against deception.
- Maintain a strong prayer life.
- Walk in faith and confidence in God's promises.

As you apply these principles, you will not only experience deliverance but also walk in divine authority, ensuring that no power of darkness can hold you bound. The same Spirit that raised Jesus from the dead dwells in you, and by Him, you have victory over every work of the enemy.

Are you ready to walk in total deliverance? The choice is yours.

WARFARE SECTION

DECREES AGAINST DEMONIC ATTACKS

Any satanic department that has captured my destiny, your time has expired, release me by force, in the name Jesus. By the power of the almighty I return every organ of my body the way God created it, in the name of Jesus. I command every demonic operation against my destiny to be terminated by the power in the blood of Jesus.

> And God said, Let us make man in our image, after our likeness: and let them have dominion over the fish of the sea, and over the fowl of the air, and over the cattle, and over all the earth, and over every creeping thing that creepeth upon the earth. So God created

> man in his own image, in the image of God created he him; male and female created he them.
>
> — GENESIS 1:26-27

You my life, rise above the manipulation of every demonic activity, in the mighty name of Jesus. I command my body, soul and spirit to align with divine image and likeness, in the name of Jesus. Any witchcraft power dominating my life, be frustrated, in the name of Jesus. Any evil power in the sea, land and other creature that has risen above me, I bring you down, in the name of Jesus. I put on the new man (Colossians 3:10) to challenge every satanic activity against my life, in the name of Jesus. Any sinful character denying me good relationship with Christ, be uprooted out of my life, in the mighty name of Jesus. Let the abundant life of Christ, peace of mind, divine prosperity locate me and move my life forward, in the name of Jesus.

> And that ye put on the new man, which after God is created in righteousness and true holiness.
>
> — EPHESIANS 4:24

> For thou hast made him a little lower than the angels, and hast crowned him with glory and honour. Thou madest him to have dominion over the works of thy

> hands; thou hast put all things under his feet: All sheep and oxen, yea, and the beasts of the field; The fowl of the air, and the fish of the sea, and whatsoever passeth through the paths of the seas. O Lord our Lord, how excellent is thy name in all the earth!
>
> — PSALMS 8:5-9

Heavenly father, renew my knowledge and wisdom to prosper without hindrance in every area of my life, in the name of Jesus. Let the angels of the living God enter into the battle field of my life and fight for me, in the name of Jesus. Holy Ghost fire, burn to ashes every demonic property in my destiny, in the name of Jesus. I bring down to nothing the evil powers behind my problems and I destroy them forever, in the mighty name of Jesus. I command my body, soul and spirit to rise in dominion above every creature. Almighty God, arise in your mercy and bless the works of my hands. Any marine spirit attack in my life, be terminated, in the mighty name of Jesus.

Ancient of days, take me away from the path of death to the path of life, in the name of Jesus. Let the excellency of God's power deliver me from every demonic attack, in the name of Jesus. Blood of Jesus, deliver me from every destructive sickness, poverty and shame. Any evil fire, kindred in any organ of my body by the devil, quench by the blood of Jesus. Any witchcraft animal tormenting my destiny in the dream or living inside me, I cut you to pieces. I break and loose myself from every demonic attack, in the name of Jesus. Any evil covenant exposing me to demonic attack, break to pieces, in the name of Jesus.

Every problem in my life forcing me to shade tears in secret or in the open, receive destruction, in the name of Jesus. Anointing to overcome every demonic attack, fall upon me, in the name of Jesus. Any satanic influence over my life to break the commandment of God, loose your hold over my life, in the mighty name of Jesus.

> And said, If thou wilt diligently hearken to the voice of the Lord thy God, and wilt do that which is right in his sight, and wilt give ear to his commandments, and keep all his statutes, I will put none of these diseases upon thee, which I have brought upon the Egyptians: for I am the Lord that healeth thee.

— EXODUS 15:26

> Submit yourselves therefore to God. Resist the devil, and he will flee from you.

— JAMES 4:7

Any evil tree, visible or invisible growing in any area of my life, be uprooted by divine thunder, in the name of Jesus. Blood of Jesus, flow into my foundation and purify my life to meet divine demand, in the name of Jesus.

Any evil force militating against my destiny, your time is up, be disgraced publicly forever, in the name of Jesus. Every problem in my life, receive divine judgment and perish, in the mighty name of Jesus. Every voice of sin or disobedience tormenting my life, be silenced by the blood of Jesus. I command every inherited bondage in my life to break to pieces, in the name of Jesus. Every property of the devil in my life, catch fire, burn to ashes and be flushed out, in the name of Jesus.

> Who forgiveth all thine iniquities; who healeth all thy diseases;
>
> — PSALMS 103:3

> When the even was come, they brought unto him many that were possessed with devils: and he cast out the spirits with his word, and healed all that were sick: That it might be fulfilled which was spoken by Esaias the prophet, saying, Himself took our infirmities, and bare our sicknesses.
>
> — MATTHEW 8:16-17

Every Egyptian disease, problems and limitation prospering in my life, receive death now, in the mighty name of Jesus. You my life begin to miscarry every weakness, evil and demonic activities in you. Lord that healeth the children of Israel, arise and heal me by fire, in the name of Jesus. Any power corrupting the waters of my life to waste my efforts in life, be wasted. By the anointing of the Holy Ghost I resist every work of the devil in my life and I command them to die, in the mighty name of Jesus.

Any evil soldier sitting upon my blessings, be unseated by death now, in the mighty name of Jesus. Problems within me and the ones without assigned to terminate divine program for my life, show up and die. Every yoke of iniquity in my life denying me of my blessings, break to pieces, in the name of Jesus. Anointing for divine health and supernatural breakthroughs, possess me now, in the name of Jesus.

I bind and cast out the spirits behind the long-time problems in my life, in the name of Jesus. By the power in the word of God, I cast out every demon in charge of my sufferings and limitations, in the name of Jesus. Every good prophesy ever said about me, receive fulfilment, in the mighty name of Jesus.

Every sickness, disease and other problem starring at my face from my place of birth, your time is up, expire, in the name of

Jesus. Any evil power threatening my destiny, I break your backbone to pieces, in the name of Jesus. Every negative utterance ever spoken against me by anyone living or dead, expire, in the name of Jesus.

> Who his own self bare our sins in his own body on the tree, that we, being dead to sins, should live unto righteousness: by whose stripes ye were healed.
>
> — 1 PETER 2:24

I command every problem in my life to be nailed in the cross of Calvary by fire, in the mighty name of Jesus. Every demonic business in my life, hear me very well, you are illegal, disappear forever, in the name of Jesus. Every dream of defeat in my life, be converted to victory by force, in the mighty name of Jesus. Every good thing that is dead in my life, receive abundant life from Christ, in the name of Jesus.

> Wherefore it shall come to pass, if ye hearken to these judgments, and keep, and do them, that the Lord thy God shall keep unto thee the covenant and the mercy which he sware unto thy fathers: And he will love thee, and bless thee, and multiply thee: he will also bless the fruit of thy womb, and the fruit of thy land, thy corn,

> and thy wine, and thine oil, the increase of thy kine, and the flocks of thy sheep, in the land which he sware unto thy fathers to give thee. Thou shalt be blessed above all people: there shall not be male or female barren among you, or among your cattle. And the Lord will take away from thee all sickness, and will put none of the evil diseases of Egypt, which thou knowest, upon thee; but will lay them upon all them that hate thee.
>
> — DEUTERONOMY 7:12-15

I stand in the righteousness of Christ and claim all my lost blessings, in the mighty name of Jesus. Let the stripes of Jesus arise in anger and kill every disease germ, infirmity and uncompromising sickness in my life, in the name of Jesus. Anointing to obey God's word, keep divine statues and covenant with God, take over my life, in the name of Jesus.

Almighty God, by your power, multiply your blessings into my life from every corner, in the mighty name of Jesus. Every inherited limit from my ancestors, I reject you now, in the mighty name of Jesus. Let the love of God begin to manifest in my life. I command every department of my life to become fruitful and to bear fruits into billions, in the name of Jesus. Divine increase and multiplication that will take me to the next level, begin to manifest, in the name of Jesus.

> And it came to pass the day after, that he went into a city called Nain; and many of his disciples went with him, and much people. Now when he came nigh to the gate of the city, behold, there was a dead man carried out, the only son of his mother, and she was a widow: and much people of the city was with her. And when the Lord saw her, he had compassion on her, and said unto her, Weep not. And he came and touched the bier: and they that bare him stood still. And he said, Young man, I say unto thee, Arise. And he that was dead sat up, and began to speak. And he delivered him to his mother.
>
> — LUKE 7:11-15

You my blessings, stand up, walk around the globe and stay above others, in the name of Jesus. Father Lord, stretch your hand and take away every sickness, disease, evil plantation and unprofitable deposits in my life. You the gates of my life, open and discharge every property of the devil in you now, in the mighty name of Jesus. Father Lord, send your son the Lord Jesus into the battle field of my life to deliver me wherever I need deliverance. Any satanic roadblock mounted against my greatness in any city, be dismantled, in the name of Jesus.

Any evil spirit following me from place to place, your time is up, leave my life alone, in the name of Jesus. Any grave digger against me, I reject you, bury your. Any demonic vessel, visible or invisible taking me away from my comfort zone, drop me by force, in the name of Jesus. Any evil eyes monitoring the best things in my life to destroy them, be blinded, in the mighty name of Jesus. Let the mercy of God deliver me from all my unrepentant enemy, in the name of Jesus. I command the spirit of death in any area of my life to be bound and cast out, in the name of Jesus.

THANK YOU!

I'd like to use this time to thank you for purchasing my books and helping my ministry and work. Any copy of my book you buy helps to fund my ministry and family, as well as offering much-needed inspiration to keep writing. My family and I are very thankful, and we take your assistance very seriously.

You have already accomplished so much, but I would appreciate an honest review of some of my books through the link below. This is critical since reviews reflect how much an author's work is respected.

Please [click here] to leave a review on Amazon. If you're viewing from a printed version, please visit amazon.com/review/create-review?asin=B0F2X56H3M to leave a review.

Please be aware that I read and value all comments and reviews. You can always post a review even though you haven't finished the book yet, and then edit your reviews later.

Thank you so much as you spare a precious moment of your time and may God bless you and meet you at the very point of your need.

You can also send me an email to hello@madueke.com if you encounter any difficulty while writing your review.

PRAYER M. MADUEKE'S BESTSELLING BOOKS

Click on any of the [Buy Now] buttons to view or purchase them on my website. If you're viewing from a printed version, please visit madueke.com and search for these books.

1.	Dictionary of Demons & Complete Deliverance	[Buy Now]
2.	Monitoring Spirits	[Buy Now]
3.	Praying with The Blood of Jesus	[Buy Now]
4.	The Power of Speaking in Tongues	[Buy Now]
5.	Speaking Things into Existence by Faith	[Buy Now]
6.	Discerning and Defeating the Ahab & Jezebel Spirit	[Buy Now]
7.	Defeating the Python Spirit	[Buy Now]
8.	35 Special Dangerous Decrees	[Buy Now]
9.	21/40 Nights of Decrees and Your Enemies Will Surrender	[Buy Now]

10. Command the Morning, Day and Night [Buy Now]
11. Evil Summon [Buy Now]
12. Overcoming & Destroying the Spirit of Rejection & Hatred [Buy Now]
13. Queen of Heaven: Wife of Satan [Buy Now]
14. The False Prophet [Buy Now]
15. Dominion Over Sickness & Disease [Buy Now]
16. The Battle Plan for Destroying Foundational Witchcraft [Buy Now]
17. The Queen of the Coast [Buy Now]
18. Dictionary of Unmerited Favor [Buy Now]
19. Prayers for Breakthrough in your Business [Buy Now]
20. A Jump From Evil Altar [Buy Now]
21. 100 Days Prayers to Wake Up Your Lazarus [Buy Now]
22. Breaking Evil Yokes [Buy Now]
23. When Evil Altars are Multiplied [Buy Now]

24. The Battle Plan for Destroying Foundational Occultism [Buy Now]

25. Prayers for Protection [Buy Now]

26. Prayers for Academic Success [Buy Now]

27. Your Dream Directory [Buy Now]

28. Prayers for Financial Breakthrough [Buy Now]

29. Destiny and Star Hunters [Buy Now]

30. Prayers to Pray during Courtship [Buy Now]

31. 91 Days Decrees to Takeover the Year [Buy Now]

32. Alone with God [Buy Now]

33. Prayers against Satanic Oppression [Buy Now]

34. Foundations Exposed [Buy Now]

35. Prayers for Deliverance [Buy Now]

36. Prayers to Heal Broken Relationship [Buy Now]

37. Prayers for Good Health [Buy Now]

38. Comprehensive Deliverance [Buy Now]

39. Prayers for College and University Students [Buy Now]

40. 40 Prayer Giants [Buy Now]

41. Divine Protection & Immunity While Sleeping [Buy Now]

42. Prayers for Fertility in your Marriage [Buy Now]

43. More Kingdoms to Conquer [Buy Now]

44. Confront and Conquer your Enemy [Buy Now]

45. Prayers to Raise Godly Children [Buy Now]

4 Free Ebooks

To say a 'Thank You' for purchasing *Deliverance from Demonic Attacks,* I offer these books to you in appreciation. Click or type **madueke.com/free-gift** in your browser.

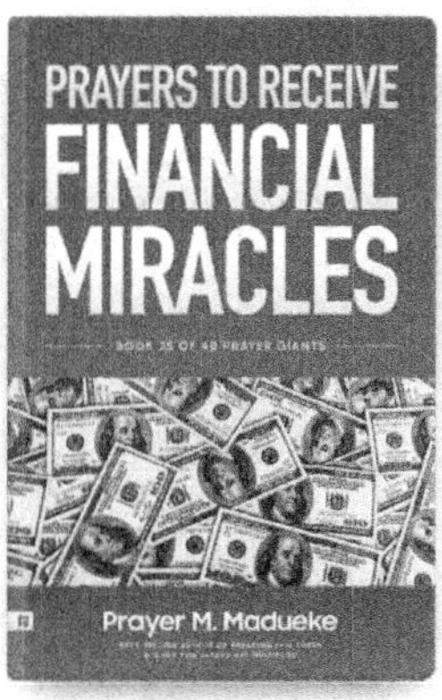

Video Access Bonus

As promised, I have prepared exclusive video content to complement the topics covered in the book you purchased. These videos offer deeper insights and discussions to enhance your learning experience.

To access this course on ***"Deliverance from Demonic Attacks,"*** for free, please follow these steps:

1. Click or type the following link into your browser: **madueke.com/courses/deliverance-from-demonic-attacks**
2. You will be directed to the course page on my website.
3. Add the course to your cart by clicking on the "**ACCESS COURSE NOW**" button and you'll be directed to the checkout page automatically.
4. On the checkout page, apply the coupon code "**demonicattacksc100off**" to get the course for free.
5. Complete the checkout process, and you will gain instant access to the course videos.

If you encounter any difficulties or have any questions, please feel free to reach out to me here: hello@madueke.com. I'm here to assist you every step of the way.

Message from the Author

I desire that you succeed, grow, and break free from negativity and obstacles. I want you to flourish, remaining resilient, and untouched by negative influences or challenging circumstances. Because of that, please permit me to introduce two courses that I believe passionately will help you:

1. To break the evil altars and powers of your father's house, The role of altars in the realm of existence is very key because altars are meeting places between the physical and the spiritual, between the visible and the invisible.

   Unless a man cuts off the evil flow from the power of his father's house, he will not fulfill his destiny. Click here to learn more about my course on how to tear down unholy altars and close the enemy's entryways into your life!

2. To help you seamlessly break iron-like problems, illness, delayed marriage, poverty, or any long-standing battle.

   Discover the transformative power of Christian fasting and prayer. Remember, Matthew 17:21 teaches us, ***"But this kind of demon does not go out except by prayer and fasting."*** Ready to overcome your struggles? Click here to learn more about this course.

Embrace the journey ahead with faith, for through prayer, fasting, and the dismantling of evil altars, you shall unlock the doors to spiritual liberation and divine breakthrough. May your path be illuminated by His grace as you walk towards a life free from bondage.

If you're seeing this from the physical copy, type the link: madueke.com/courses in your browser to view all the courses on my website.

Prayer Madueke

CHRISTIAN AUTHOR

Christian Counseling

We were created for a greater purpose than only survival and God wants us to live a full life.

If you need prayer or counseling or have any other inquiries, please visit the counseling page on my website to find out when I am available for a phone call.

Click or type links.madueke.com/counseling in your browser.

Let's Connect on Youtube

Join me on my YouTube channel, "Prayer M. Madueke," where I share powerful insights, guidance, and prayers for spiritual breakthroughs.

Subscribe today to unlock the secrets of the Kingdom and embrace an abundant life. Let's grow together!

Click or type links.madueke.com/youtube in your browser.

An Invitation to Become a Ministry Partner

I appreciate the support and inquiries I have received regarding collaboration with my ministry. Your prayers and dedication to the work of the Kingdom are highly valued.

You can also visit the donation page on my website if you would like to contribute or learn more about supporting my ministry: madueke.com/donate.

Thank you for your continued support and faithfulness in Christ Jesus.